Today is a Windy Day

by Martha E. H. Rustad

raintree

a Capstone company — publishers for children

Raintree is an imprint of Capstone Global Library Limited, a company incorporated in England and Wales having its registered office at 264 Banbury Road, Oxford, OX2 7DY – Registered company number: 6695582

www.raintree.co.uk
myorders@raintree.co.uk

Text © Capstone Global Library Limited 2017
The moral rights of the proprietor have been asserted.

Edited by Marissa Kirkman
Designed by Charmaine Whitman and Peggie Carley
Picture research by Tracey Engel
Production by Katy LaVigne
Originated by Capstone Global Library
Printed and bound in China.

ISBN 978 1 4747 3875 0
20 19 18 17 16
10 9 8 7 6 5 4 3 2 1

British Library Cataloguing in Publication Data
A full catalogue record for this book is available from the British Library.

Acknowledgements
We would like to thank the following for permission to reproduce photographs: Getty Images: Cultura RM Exclusive/Moof, 8 (bottom), JGI/Daniel Grill, 1, 8 (top); Shutterstock: AlexLinck, 14 (top), andreiuc88, 12; best4u, 6 (compass), Chalermpon Poungpeth, 4, Kseniia Neverkovska, cover and interior design element, Gazlast, 6 (map), Rob Wilson, 14 (bottom), Robnroll, 16, Sergey Novikov, cover, 20, ShaunWilkinson, 10, signet, cover and interior design element, ssuaphotos, 18

Contents

What is the weather like?

Today is a windy day.

The air moves on a windy day.

Let's find out how windy it is.

Today's wind speeds (mph)

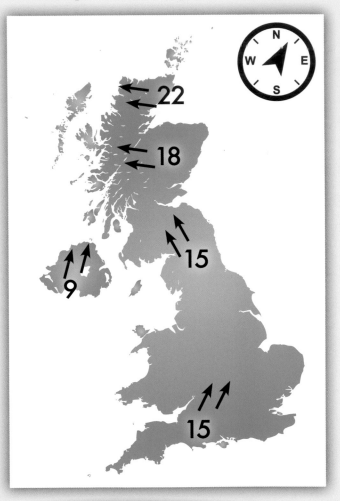

We look at the forecast.
The numbers tell us how
fast the wind will blow.
The arrows tell us the
wind direction.

summer

winter

8

The wind can blow for many days.

Windy days happen in any season.

Warm air blows in the summer.

Cold air blows in the winter.

What do we see?

We cannot see the wind.

But we can see what the wind moves.

Clouds move quickly across the sky.

Sometimes the wind brings rain clouds.

We see grass and leaves

move in a light wind.

A light wind is called a breeze.

Your hair blows around in the breeze.

Strong winds called gales can bend tree trunks. We see branches move in a strong wind. Flags move a lot on very windy days.

What do we do?

We hang wet clothes outside.

Shirts and trousers flap in the wind.

The wind dries out our clothes.

We watch a wind turbine turn.

The wind moves its blades.

This wind energy is turned

into electricity.

We fly a kite on a windy day.

The kite soars above us.

Can we fly a kite tomorrow?

Let's check the forecast.

Glossary

electricity a form of energy

forecast prediction of what the weather will be

pattern several things that are repeated in the same way each time

turbine machine that creates electricity

Find out more

Books

Finding Out about Wind Energy (What Are Energy Sources?), Matt Doeden (Lerner Classroom, 2015)

What Is Wind? (Unseen Science), Linda Ivancic (Cavendish Square, 2016)

Wind (Weather Watch), Jenny Fretland VanVoorst (Bullfrog Books, 2017)

Websites

www.eia.gov/kids/energy.cfm?page=wind_home-basics
Learn about the history of wind power and how wind turbines work.

www.sciencenewsforstudents.org/article/cool-jobs-power-wind
Learn about jobs that study the wind and watch a video on wind turbines.

climatekids.nasa.gov
Learn about the Earth's climate with games and videos.

Index

Note to parents and teachers

The What is the Weather Today? series supports National Curriculum requirements for science related to weather. This book describes and illustrates a windy day. The images support early readers in understanding the text. The repetition of words and phrases helps early readers learn new words. This book also introduces early readers to subject-specific vocabulary words, which are defined in the Glossary section. Early readers may need assistance to read some words and to use the Contents, Glossary, Find out more and Index sections of the book.